THE Best Hikes OF THE Twin Cities

by Kate Havelin

Adventure Publications, Inc.
Cambridge, MN

ACKNOWLEDGMENTS

This book is dedicated to the countless people who work to preserve and maintain the many city, county, regional, and state parks in the Twin Cities. Our community is richer because of the vision and efforts of people like Minneapolis's great park superintendent, Theodore Wirth, who posted signs that read, "Please Walk on the Grass," and others like him, such as the Works Progress Administration crews of the 1930s, who built the fine stone bridges and buildings we enjoy at many parks. And we can't forget all the people who are working to protect and maintain our parks today, including those who support the "Vote Yes for Minnesota" campaign, which seeks dedicated funding to preserve our state's natural habitats. The land, lakes, and rivers they preserve are a gift to us all.

I'd also like to thank the helpful folks at Adventure Publications, including Gerri Slabaugh; Ryan Jacobson, who made easy-to-use maps from the jumble of information I sent him; and especially editor Brett Ortler, who shaped this book and made the writing flow.

Edited by Brett Ortler
Cover and book design by Jonathan Norberg and Karly Hanson
Trail maps by Ryan Jacobson

Photos by Brenna Slabaugh

10 9 8 7 6 5 4 3 2 1

Copyright 2008 by Kate Havelin
Published by Adventure Publications, Inc.
820 Cleveland Street S
Cambridge, MN 55008
800-678-7006
www.adventurepublications.net

ISBN-13: 978-1-59193-089-1
ISBN-10: 1-59193-089-8

TABLE OF CONTENTS

Introduction

Best Hikes of the Twin Cities

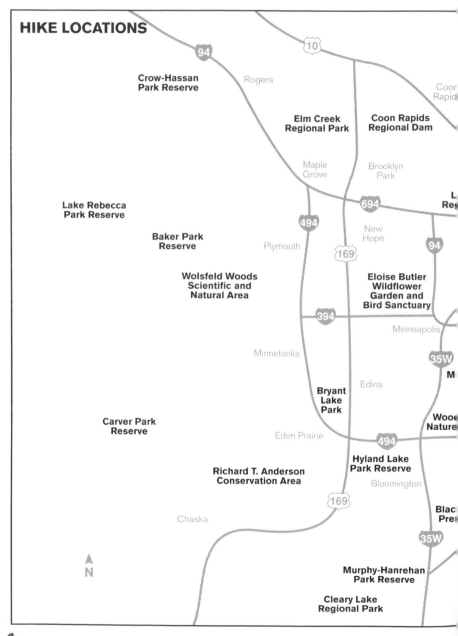

HIKE LOCATIONS

Crow-Hassan
Park Reserve

Rogers

Coon
Rapid

94

10

Elm Creek
Regional Park

Coon Rapids
Regional Dam

Maple
Grove

Brooklyn
Park

694

L
Re

Lake Rebecca
Park Reserve

494

New
Hope

94

Baker Park
Reserve

Plymouth

169

Wolsfeld Woods
Scientific and
Natural Area

Eloise Butler
Wildflower
Garden and
Bird Sanctuary

394

Minneapolis

Minnetonka

35W

M

Edina

Bryant
Lake
Park

Carver Park
Reserve

Eden Prairie

494

Woo
Nature

Hyland Lake
Park Reserve

Richard T. Anderson
Conservation Area

Bloomington

169

Chaska

Blac
Pres

35W

A
N

Murphy-Hanrehan
Park Reserve

Cleary Lake
Regional Park

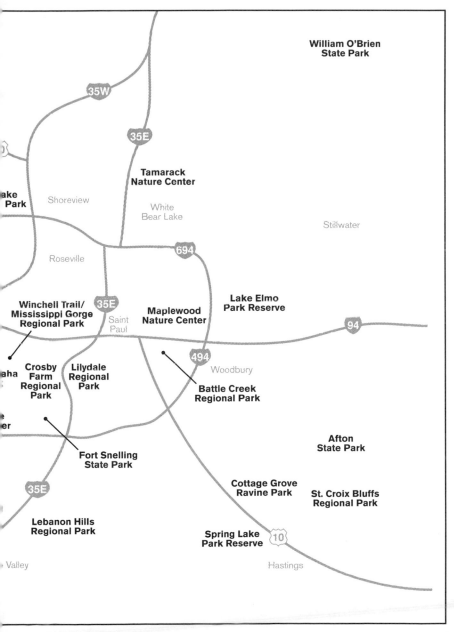

William O'Brien
State Park

35W

35E

Tamarack
Nature Center

Shoreview

White
Bear Lake

Stillwater

ake
Park

Roseville

694

35E

Lake Elmo
Park Reserve

Winchell Trail/
Mississippi Gorge
Regional Park

Saint
Paul

Maplewood
Nature Center

94

aha

Crosby
Farm
Regional
Park

Lilydale
Regional
Park

494

Woodbury

Battle Creek
Regional Park

er

Afton
State Park

Fort Snelling
State Park

35E

Cottage Grove
Ravine Park

St. Croix Bluffs
Regional Park

Lebanon Hills
Regional Park

Spring Lake
Park Reserve

10

Valley

Hastings

EVERYONE CAN HIKE

This book is for anyone who likes to get outside and hike. It's easier than you think to go hiking—you don't need a lot of special gear, and you don't need to load up the car, fill the gas tank, and drive for hours to find beautiful places to explore. The Twin Cities are endowed with countless parks and nature reserves rich with natural beauty, and many of them are right around the corner.

Most hikers have their biases. Some prefer flat trails, or trails with lots of hills. I prefer unpaved trails, and I don't like to share my trails with horses or mountain bikers, so in this book I often focus on trails that are unpaved and consist of dirt or grass. With that said, many parks have wonderful paved trails. Don't hesitate to check them all out; there are more than enough to go around.

In fact, there are more Twin Cities trails than I could possibly include, so I had to be choosy. I did my best to include a variety of trails from throughout the area, but some areas have more trails than others. For instance, there are fewer trails in the southeast metro and more in the southwest; that's just where the trails are.

Many trails are clustered along the Mississippi River. The Twin Cities grew around the river, so it's fitting that our parks have grown up around this monumental river as well. Thanks to conservation efforts, the river is cleaner now than it was fifty years ago, and as the Twin Cities continue to grow, this reclaimed green space becomes even more precious. The trails are great for hiking; in fact, the riverfront trails of Minneapolis and St. Paul represent the best of urban hiking.

I also write about trails that are clustered close together in the suburbs, but every trail I suggest is unique. For instance, Baker Park Reserve and the Wolsfeld Woods Scientific and Natural Area are geographically close together, but they're very different places. The Baker Reserve is known primarily as recreation area and loaded with amenities, whereas the Wolsfeld Natural Area is a great example of the "Big Woods," and doesn't have any extras or amenities. The same goes for Murphy-Hanrehan Park Reserve and Cleary Lake Regional Park; they are practically next-door neighbors, but each offers different hiking experiences. Cleary's flat terrain makes for easy walking; Murphy Park is rugged and extremely hilly.

No matter what kind of trail you like, chances are you can find it somewhere in the metro area. And I've included a series of lists for those of you interested in a certain type of hiking: parks with biking trails, trails that are good for bird watching and wildflowers, as well as trails for those of you looking for hills, night hikes, or winter hikes. And on page 9, I listed my Top Ten Hikes. These are my personal favorites and are the best trails I think the Cities have to offer.

WHAT TO BRING: NO BACKPACK REQUIRED

When you think of hiking, you might conjure an image of a backpacker wearing heavy hiking boots and carrying a hulking backpack stuffed with a sleeping bag, a tent, and loads of gear. But you don't need to weigh yourself down with so much stuff to go hiking. You can travel light. Here's what I suggest you bring for the hikes in this book:

Decent shoes

You don't need fancy hiking boots, but it makes sense to wear shoes, sneakers, or boots that give your feet some support and are comfortable.

Water, and a snack

How much water and food you need to bring depends on how long you'll be hiking. I think it's smart to bring a bottle of water anytime you'll be hiking for an hour or more. (In hot weather, I carry water with me all the time, even on short hikes.) I like having my hands free, so I stash my water bottle in a waist belt that has a small pouch for a snack, money, keys, and a map. Of course, pockets, a small backpack, or your hands will do the trick too.

Seasonal clothing

Baseball hats with a brim offer protection from sun and rain. I often bring at least a lightweight extra layer—a thin long-sleeved shirt, fleece, or a rain jacket—that I wear if the weather changes when I'm hiking. It's easy enough to tie that extra layer around your waist, or fit it in a small backpack.

Map

Many of the parks in this book have maps posted along the trail, but it's a good idea to carry a map with you. Be sure to get an official map from the park, as this book will not show every park trail in detail. Maps weigh almost nothing, but they may keep you from getting lost, or worrying about where you are on the trail.

Depending on which trail you're hiking, how long you'll be out, and your personal preference, you may also want to carry some of these optional items as well:

- compass
- food
- first aid
- guidebooks about trails, flora, fauna
- bug repellent
- camera
- cell phone

Before you go: Use sunscreen!

My family members roll their eyes at my insistence on sunscreen, but protecting skin is a necessity. More than a million people are diagnosed with skin cancer each year; that's a one in five chance over a lifetime, according to the American Academy of Dermatology. Sunscreen isn't just for sunny summer days. People can get sunburned on overcast days and even in winter when sun reflects off snow. Take it from two-time Cy Young winner and former Minnesota Twins pitcher Johan Santana, who says, "Skin cancer doesn't care how light or dark you are. Everyone is at risk. Use sunscreen." (www.playsmartsun.org)

Kate's Top Ten Hiking Trails

I like every trail in this book, but some places are exceptional. For what it's worth, here's my list of the ten best Twin Cities hiking trails:

Afton State Park, Hastings, page 18
Afton's sweeping prairies, wooded ravines, and scenic river trails provide thrills for all kinds of hikers.

Black Dog Preserve, Burnsville, page 24
This is an untamed oasis in the middle of the metro area. Here, you can see what Minnesota was like hundreds of years ago.

Crosby Farm Regional Park, St. Paul, page 36
Crosby is the Twin Cities' best place to see the Mississippi River in all seasons. The trails are flat, easy, and above all, accessible.

Crow-Hassan Park Reserve, Rogers, page 38
This rustic park brings to mind Little House on the Prairie. The miles of prairie make it seem more like you're on the frontier than near a city.

Eloise Butler Wildflower Garden, Minneapolis, page 42
Simply put, this garden seems like a movie setting, and one set in the middle of a major metropolis.

Murphy-Hanrehan Park Reserve, Savage, page 62
Come here for the hills. The climbs are steep and make for great hiking.

Richard T. Anderson Conservation Area, Eden Prairie, page 64
I can't wait to hike here again. I was swept away by the woods, prairie grassland and challenging hills.

Spring Lake Park Reserve, Hastings, page 66
The Mississippi River doesn't look like this anywhere else. In part of the park, the river spans a mile across. In another, the Mississippi looks more like the Boundary Waters than a river. Visit both sections, you won't be disappointed.

Winchell Trail/Mississippi River Gorge, Minneapolis, page 74
From Lake Itasca to New Orleans, this is the Mississippi's only gorge. The Winchell Trail is close to my home and close to my heart, and it's a place you should know.

Wolsfeld Woods Scientific and Natural Area, Orono, page 76
If you want to see the "Big Woods," this is the place to go. When I close my eyes and imagine deep, beautiful woods, this is the picture I see.

SPECIAL INTEREST HIKES

Good trails for . . .
Night • Hills • Easy • Birding • Wildflowers • Winter • Rivers • Bikes

Night Hikes

These Three Rivers Park District Parks light some trails in spring and fall for their "Walk When the Moon is Full" night hike programs. Check www.threeriversparks.org for specifics.

Hilly Hikes

Easy Hikes

Maplewood Nature Center, Maplewood, page 58
Spring Lake Park Reserve, Hastings, page 66
Tamarack Nature Center, White Bear Township, page 70
Winchell Trail/Mississippi Gorge, Minneapolis, page 74
Wood Lake Nature Center, Richfield, page 78

Birding Hikes

Black Dog Preserve, Burnsville, page 24
Crosby Farm Regional Park, St. Paul, page 36
Crow-Hassan Park Reserve, Rogers, page 38
Eloise Butler Wildflower Garden, Minneapolis, page 42
Fort Snelling State Park, Minneapolis, page 44
Lake Rebecca Park Reserve, Independence, page 50
Lilydale Regional Park, St. Paul, page 54
Maplewood Nature Center, Maplewood, page 58
Murphy-Hanrehan Park Reserve, Savage, page 62
Tamarack Nature Center, White Bear Township, page 70
William O'Brien State Park, Marine on St. Croix, page 72
Wood Lake Nature Center, Richfield, page 78

Wildflower Hikes

Black Dog Preserve, Burnsville, page 24
Crow-Hassan Park Reserve, Rogers, page 38
Eloise Butler Wildflower Garden, Minneapolis, page 42
Long Lake Regional Park, New Brighton, page 56
Murphy-Hanrehan Park Reserve, Savage, page 62
Wolsfeld Woods Scientific and Natural Area, Long Lake, page 76

Winter Hikes

These parks offer some plowed walking or snowshoe trails. Several parks rent snowshoes.

Afton State Park, Hastings, page 18
Carver Park Reserve, Victoria, page 28

River Hikes
Crow River

Minnesota River

Mississippi River

St. Croix River

Bike Trails

Many parks include some biking trails, some of which may be shared with hikers. The parks marked by asterisks have mountain bike trails.

*Afton State Park, Hastings, page 18

*Battle Creek Regional Park, St. Paul, page 22

Crosby Farm Regional Park, St. Paul, page 36

Elm Creek Regional Park, Maple Grove, page 40

Hyland Lake Park Reserve, Bloomington, page 46

*Lake Elmo Park Reserve, Lake Elmo, page 48

*Lake Rebecca Park Reserve, Independence, page 50

*Lebanon Hills Regional Park, Eagan-Apple Valley, page 52

Lilydale Regional Park, St. Paul, page 54

Minnehaha Park, Minneapolis, page 60 (the popular Minnehaha bike trails run through and around the park)

*Murphy-Hanrehan Park Reserve, Savage, page 62

Bringing Your Dog Along

Bringing your dog to a park can make a good hike even more fun, and many of the parks listed in this book are dog-friendly. There are exceptions, of course. Scientific and Natural Areas, and most nature centers don't allow dogs.

Of the many parks that allow dogs, each has its own rules. Often, some trails are open to dogs, and others aren't. For instance, some parks have hike-only trails, whereas other parks have trails that are shared with dogs, hikers, and horses. The same goes for specific areas of certain parks. (At Black Dog Preserve, for example, dogs are allowed on some trails, but not in the southwest section of the park, which is a Scientific and Natural Area.)

So be sure to familiarize yourself with park rules before heading out, as it can save you time and inconvenience. Often, such rules can be found online, or by simply giving the park a phone call.

Some parks offer off-leash dog parks. In addition, most off-leash dog parks have rules of their own, and some have areas that are reserved for small dogs only, whereas, in others, small dogs and large dogs roam together. And if you're going to a dog park, chances are you'll need your purse or wallet; dog parks often charge a nominal fee for use of the park. Some parks even offer "season passes." The parks listed below offer dog parks or there are dog parks nearby; be sure to check them out.

Battle Creek Regional Park, Maplewood, page 22

Bryant Lake Regional Park, Eden Prairie, page 26

Carver Park Reserve, Victoria, page 28

Cleary Lake Regional Park, Prior Lake, page 30

Crosby Farm Regional Park, St. Paul, page 36
(Across the river in Minneapolis is the Minnehaha Off-Leash Recreation Area, where permits are required.)

Crow-Hassan Park Reserve, Rogers, page 38

Elm Creek Regional Park, Maple Grove, page 40

Lake Rebecca Park Reserve, Independence, page 50
(the off-leash area is at nearby Lake Sarah)

Lebanon Hills Regional Park, Eagan and Apple Valley, page 52
(Dakota Woods Dog Park is further south, at County road 46 and
Blaine Avenue in Coates.)

Long Lake Regional Park, New Brighton, page 56
(Northwest of this park is an Off-Leash Area at the Rice Creek
North Regional Trail on County Road J.)

Minnehaha Park, Minneapolis, page 60

Tamarack Nature Center, White Bear Township, page 70
(Ramsey County has an off-leash dog area north of the nature
center by Otter Lake.)

Winchell Trail/Mississippi Gorge Regional Park, St. Paul, page 74
(Not far south, at 54th Street and Minnehaha, is the Minnehaha
off-leash dog area.)

Above all, if you're bringing your dog to one of the parks listed in
this book, use common sense. Most parks require you to have your
dog on a leash (and some will issue fines if rules are violated) and all
parks require you to clean up after your dog, so please be consider-
ate and respect other park users, whether they have dogs, are riding
horses, or are just going for a good hike. Although dogs are almost
never allowed in park buildings, many parks are fairly dog friendly, so
get your furry friend leashed up, get your hiking shoes on, and get
out there!

For more detailed information, see the chart on the next page. I've
compiled information about all of the parks, including those with
dog parks, those that allow dogs on specific trails, and parks where
dogs aren't allowed.

HIKING WITH DOGS

	Dogs Not Allowed	Dogs Allowed on Specific Trails
Afton State Park		●
Baker Park Reserve		●
Battle Creek Regional Park		●
Black Dog Preserve		●
Bryant Lake Regional Park		●
Carver Park Reserve		●
Cleary Lake Regional Park		●
Coon Rapids Dam Regional Park		●
Cottage Grove Ravine Park		●
Crosby Farm Regional Park		●
Crow-Hassan Park Reserve		●
Elm Creek Regional Park		●
Eloise Butler Wildflower Garden	●	
Fort Snelling State Park		●
Hyland Lake Park Reserve		●
Lake Elmo Park Reserve		●
Lake Rebecca Park Reserve		●
Lebanon Hills Regional Park		●
Lilydale Regional Park		●
Long Lake Regional Park		●
Maplewood Nature Center	●	
Minnehaha Park		●
Murphy-Hanrehan Park Reserve		●
Richard T. Anderson Conservation Area		●
Spring Lake Park Reserve		●
St. Croix Bluffs Regional Park		●
Tamarack Nature Center	●	
William O'Brien State Park		●
Winchell Trail/Mississippi Gorge		●
Wolsfeld Woods SNA	●	
Wood Lake Nature Center	●	

Off-leash Dog Park on Premises	Notes
	Dogs must be leashed and picked up after.
	Dogs allowed only on designated trails.
●	Dog park on premises; must be leashed elsewhere.
	Dogs not allowed in southwest section of park.
●	Dogs allowed on designated trails, not on the beach.
●	Dogs must be leashed, picked up after; dog park.
●	Dogs must be leashed and picked up after.
	Dogs allowed on designated trails; must be leashed.
	Dogs are not allowed on trails when there is snow.
	Dogs must be leashed and picked up after.
●	Dog park on premises; allowed on designated trails.
●	Dogs allowed only in designated areas and dog park.
	No dogs allowed.
	Dogs must be leashed and picked up after.
	Dogs allowed on designated trails.
	Dogs allowed on designated trails.
	Must be leashed, picked up after; dog park nearby.
	Must be leashed, picked up after; dog park nearby.
	Must be leashed and picked up after.
	Must be leashed and picked up after.
	No dogs allowed.
●	Dogs must be leashed and picked up after; dog park.
	Dogs allowed only on designated trails.
	Dogs must be leashed and picked up after.
	Dogs must be leashed and picked up after.
	No dogs at the beach, campgrounds or picnic shelter.
	No dogs allowed.
	Dogs must be leashed and picked up after.
	Dogs must be leashed and picked up after.
	No dogs allowed.
	No dogs allowed.

Afton State Park

WHERE
Hastings

DIRECTIONS
From Interstate 94, head south on State Highway 95. Turn left and head east on County Road 20. Follow the signs to the park. Park in the visitor center parking lot.

OVERVIEW
The park's almost 1,700 acres attract hikers, boaters, campers, horseback riders, bicyclists, trail runners, as well as winter sports enthusiasts.

RECOMMENDED TRAILS
From the visitor center, hikers can head north toward the St. Croix River or go west through the woods toward Afton Alps. Either way, the trails lead north and west up to the prairie. Here, hikers can walk along wide, grassy trails over the rolling bluff lands.

TERRAIN
This is a hilly park. From the visitor center trailheads, hikers proceed down long hills to reach the flat river bottom trails or the dirt trails below Afton Alps. Other steep hills lead up and down the prairie and through the woods.

OTHER TRAILS
Past the prairie, the park's west side slopes through a lovely wooded ravine, where hikers can opt to hike a 1.4-mile loop. There is also an additional short prairie loop and snowshoe trails that meander south and west through the woods and past a small creek.

FACILITIES

bathrooms	gift shop	vending machine
benches	shelters	visitor center
camping	solar pump	water fountains
exhibits	vault toilets	

COST

state park permit required

CONTACTS

Afton State Park, 651-436-5391 or www.dnr.state.mn.us/state_parks

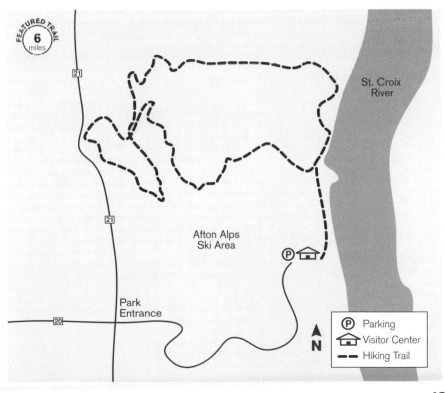

Baker Park Reserve

SURFACE: dirt, woodchip, grass, paved

WHERE

Maple Plain

DIRECTIONS

From Highway 12, take County Road 29 north to County Road 19. Go north on County Road 19 to the park entrance. To reach the hiking-only trails, continue past the park entrance, then turn east on County Road 24. Drive past the Marshview Group Camp, then turn left at the second driveway, which is the hiking-only trailhead.

OVERVIEW

This 2,700-acre park includes several lakes, the Near-Wilderness Settlement, and Baker National Golf Course. Baker is a full-service park, with many amenities clustered around the main park entrance at Lake Independence.

RECOMMENDED TRAILS

Baker offers almost twenty miles of hiking trails, but the 2.5 miles of hiking-only trails at the Marshview Group Camp stand out. To get there, start at the hiking-only trailhead east of the Marshview Group Camp. From the trailhead, hikers can explore the Timber and Hill Trails. The 1.2-mile Timber Trail offers marvelous views of marshland and lovely expanses of grasses, reeds, and ferns.

TERRAIN

The 1.3-mile Hill Trail includes rolling hills and a fairly moderate climb. Many of the other trails are gently rolling.

OTHER TRAILS

The six miles of trails around Lake Katrina offer a fine view, but some of the trails are heavily pocked with horse tracks. The beach, playground, and campsites at the main park entrance draw many visitors, so those paved trails feel crowded at times. Other trailheads are shared with horses, dogs, or bikes.

FACILITIES

bathrooms		
beach	concessions	playground
boat launch	fishing pier	water fountains
boat/bike rentals	golf course	winter sports
camping	picnic areas	

COST

free

CONTACTS

Baker Park main gate, 763-479-2473 or www.threeriversparks.org

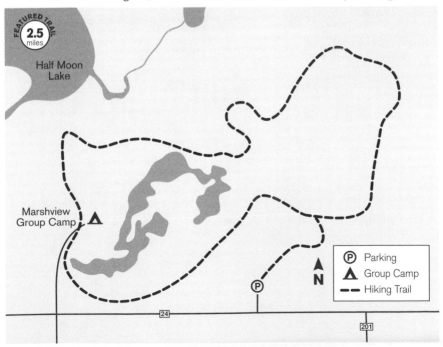

FEATURED TRAIL
2.5 miles

Half Moon Lake

Marshview Group Camp

Ⓟ Parking
▲ Group Camp
- - Hiking Trail

N

24

201

Battle Creek Regional Park

SURFACE: dirt, woodchip, grass, paved

WHERE

St. Paul

DIRECTIONS

To reach the Winthrop Street trails from Highway 61 in St. Paul, head south to Lower Afton Road and turn left. Go east to Winthrop Street, then turn left into the parking lot.

OVERVIEW

Named for an 1842 skirmish between Dakota and Ojibwe tribes, this Ramsey County park is a welcome slice of woodland surrounded by houses and busy roads. Battle Creek is a true urban park—woodlands in a city.

RECOMMENDED TRAILS

Hikers who walk the Winthrop Street trails will lope up and down many hills and pass nearby homes and apartments. At times, the trails skirt alongside roads and overlook Highway 61.

The Winthrop Street trail crosses Battle Creek Road to Battle Creek's west trails. Those west trails include 4 kilometers of easy ski trails, plus a challenging mountain bike trail that ends at a paved path leading to the Point Douglas Road trailhead. The Lower Afton Road dog park trails meander in loops, just the way dogs roam.

TERRAIN

The Winthrop trails include plenty of moderate-to-steep hills; the Lower Afton dog park trails are milder. In winter, many of the trails are groomed for skiers. Most of the Point Douglas and Edgewater Boulevard trails are paved.

OTHER TRAILS

Battle Creek includes nine miles of trails, which are mostly grass, dirt, and woodchips. Battle Creek has five trailheads: Winthrop Street, Upper Afton Road, Lower Afton Road, Point Douglas Road, and Edgewater Boulevard.

FACILITIES

free lockers
golf course
mountain biking
off-leash dog area

picnic shelter
playground
rec center (closed weekends)

snacks/pop
water fountains

COST

free

CONTACTS

Ramsey County Parks 651-748-2500 or www.co.ramsey.mn.us/parks

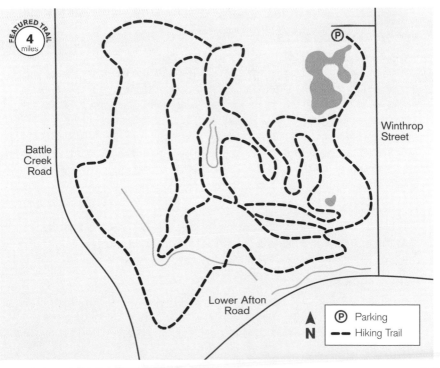

FEATURED TRAIL
4 miles

Battle Creek Road

Winthrop Street

Lower Afton Road

Ⓟ Parking
- - Hiking Trail

Black Dog Preserve

SURFACE: dirt, woodchip, grass

WHERE
Burnsville

DIRECTIONS
From Interstate 35W, take Cliff Road (exit 4A) and travel east under the freeway. Continue east one mile, then turn left into a parking lot that's used for the preserve, Cliff Fen Park, and a Park-and-Ride.

OVERVIEW
The 1,400-acre preserve encompasses a rare calcium-rich fen and wet prairie. Water defines the park and flows year-round. In fact, some low-lying areas flood here in spring. In summer, the fen's alkaline groundwater is just below the soil surface; the mix of calcium and magnesium rich groundwater allows more than a half-dozen rare kinds of plants to thrive.

RECOMMENDED TRAILS
Once you've turned into the Cliff Fen Park parking lot, park on the east side, by the soccer field. A wooden kiosk marks the Cliff Fen Park trailhead. From here, hikers can cross the train tracks and step into a wild world. Although the trail is just two miles long, the scenery along the way varies considerably. Hikers pass prairie, fen, marsh, lake, and woodland. The open water allows some waterfowl to stay here for much of the winter. Waterfowl, birds, and wildflowers are easy to spot. Willow flycatchers, orchard orioles, double-breasted cormorants, and ringed-necked pheasants make this a bird-watcher's haven.

TERRAIN
There is only one slight hill from the trailhead down past the train tracks. At the trailhead, hikers climb 53 steps to cross over one set of railroad tracks separating the trailhead parking area from the trail.

OTHER TRAILS
Another trailhead, by Black Dog Park, is farther east on Territorial Drive by 19th Avenue South. This two-mile, skinny, lumpy trail of dirt, grass, and some rocks is framed by many tall, scratchy plants. Long pants are a good idea here.

FACILITIES

ball field
picnic tables | seasonal water | vault toilet

COST

free

CONTACTS

Minnesota Valley National Wildlife Refuge, 952-854-5900, or http://fws. gov/midwest/minnesotavalley and http://www.dnr.state.mn.us/snas

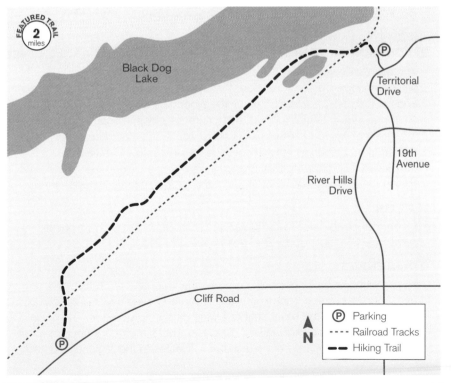

SURFACE: dirt, grass, woodchip, paved

WHERE
Eden Prairie

DIRECTIONS
From Crosstown Highway 62, go south on Shady Oak Road to Rowland Road and turn right. Proceed west on Rowland then turn left into the park. To reach the off-leash dog park, continue straight on Rowland for .5 mile, then turn left into the parking lot.

OVERVIEW
Wedged amid suburban development and sprawling highways, this park packs a surprising number of amenities into a small space. Though closed from November to March 30, the park revolves around Bryant Lake and water-related activities.

RECOMMENDED TRAILS
The main trailhead is near the park's entrance. The trail leads past two small wetlands, over a gravel road, then across a boardwalk. The grass trail ends at the park's eastern edge, by the Wooddale Church and Highway 212. The park's .8-mile turf trail isn't a complete loop; it connects to 1.7-miles of paved trails that hikers share with bikers and dogs. From the eastern park border, hikers can continue walking south and west on a paved trail. This paved trail winds past private homes. Soon, hikers can spot Bryant Lake, along with many views of the opulent homes along its shore.

TERRAIN
Moderate rolling hills. A 95-step staircase leads to the park's highest point, the 10th hole of the disc golf course.

OTHER TRAILS
Hikers who want a longer walk can continue west and north from the beach for an out-and-back walk along a shared paved trail. Hikers can continue north on the paved trail or a wide dirt and gravel trail. The gravel trail ends before the Highway 62 overpass. That's the park's boundary, but the paved trail continues on for another 1.5 miles to the regional LRT trail.

Park Highlight!

This compact park is ideal for a picnic or a day by the water. Bryant Lake's beach is the heart of this suburban park; kayaks, paddle boats, and rowboats are available here for rent.

FACILITIES

beach
boat launch
concession stand
disc golf course
fishing pier
off-leash dog park

pavilions
picnic areas
playground
public phone

restrooms
water fountains
watercraft rentals
wheelchair-accessible

COST

free, but $5 for the dog park

CONTACTS

Bryant Lake Regional Park, 763-694-7764 or
www.threeriversparkdistrict.org.

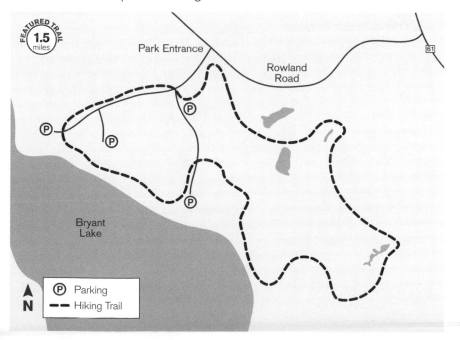

Carver Park Reserve

SURFACE: dirt, woodchip, boardwalk

WHERE
Victoria

DIRECTIONS
From Highway 494, take Highway 5 west for thirteen miles, then turn right and head north on County Road 11 (Victoria Drive) just past the Dairy Queen. Turn right at the entrance to Lowry Nature Center and park by the nature center.

OVERVIEW
Carver's motto is "Wetlands and Woods" and this perfectly suits the range of rolling hills, tamarack swamp, and maple-oak woods that grace the park's 3,500 acres. Carver's 18-plus miles of pleasant and wide trails are dirt, woodchip, and some boardwalk. This Three Rivers Parks District reserve features the Twin Cities' first public nature center, built in 1968-69.

RECOMMENDED TRAILS
The main trailhead is at the Lowry Nature Center. The trails from the nature center range over mellow hills and meander past woods and water. Long boardwalks traverse lakes, marshes, and tamarack bogs, making it easy for hikers to be in the wetlands without getting wet feet. Here, expanses of cattails and tall grasses ripple like waves.

TERRAIN
Rolling hills but nothing really steep.

OTHER TRAILS
To reach the Grimm Road trailhead, continue north on County Road 11, then turn left on Grimm Road. The Grimm Road trailhead is closed in winter. The Tamarack Trail features the flattest section of Carver Park. Carver's woods and waters are habitat for more than 100 species of birds, including loon, killdeer, osprey, and marsh wren. A sign here notes that Carver is one of the few places tamaracks grow in the metro area. Tamaracks are a tree with deep ties to the past. Native Americans used the trees' strong root fibers to sew their birch bark canoes. As the area becomes drier, aspen and dogwood are replacing the tamaracks.

FACILITIES

- bathrooms
- boat launch
- camping
- exhibits
- fishing pier

- nature center
- off-leash dog park
- picnic area
- play area

- sledding hill
- snowshoe rental
- water fountains

COST

free

CONTACTS

Carver Park Reserve, 952-472-4911 or www.threeriversparkdistrict.org

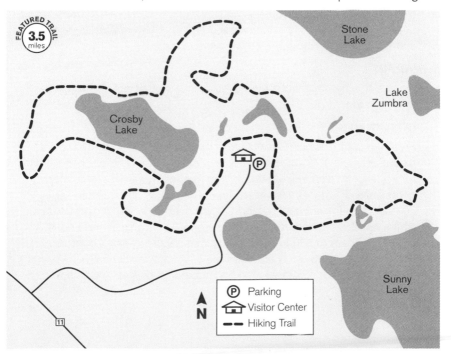

Cleary Lake Regional Park

SURFACE: dirt, woodchip, boardwalk, paved

WHERE

Prior Lake

DIRECTIONS

From Highway 169, take Highway 13 south to County Road 42. Go east on 42 to County Road 27 and follow 27 south to the park entrance.

OVERVIEW

Cleary Lake's golfing, camping, water sports, off-leash dog park, and trails attract many visitors to this pleasant park.

RECOMMENDED TRAILS

The trailheads for the scenic Poplar Creek hike-only trail and the paved bike-hike trails are just across the park road from the visitor center. The Poplar Creek Trail glides past a winding creek and wild apple trees, pines, cedars, and wetlands vary the wooded scene. This wide trail is lit in spring and fall for hikers and in winter for skiers.

TERRAIN

No real hills here, although the paved bike-hike trail includes a few gentle rolling inclines.

OTHER TRAILS

From the south trailhead, hikers can walk west on the 2.25-mile, paved bike-hike trail that loops around the lake's west side. The trail bends past thick stands of pine trees that give way to a rolling savanna and offers good views of Cleary Lake. At the lake's west side, the trail rolls past several boulders, remnants of the glaciers that once swept over this land. At the lake's north end, the paved bike-hike trail is also open to dogs. The paved trail leads to a turf hike-dog trail that parallels noisy County Road 21. That 1.2-mile turf trail also doubles as a snowmobile trail. The paved bike-hike-dog trail continues east and south around the beach area.

FACILITIES

beach
bike/boat rentals
camping
exhibit area
fishing pier
golf course
off-leash dog area

picnic areas
playground
restrooms
vending machine

visitor center
water fountains

COST

free; fee for dog park

CONTACTS

Cleary Lake Regional Park office, 763-694-7777 or
www.threeriversparkdistrict.org

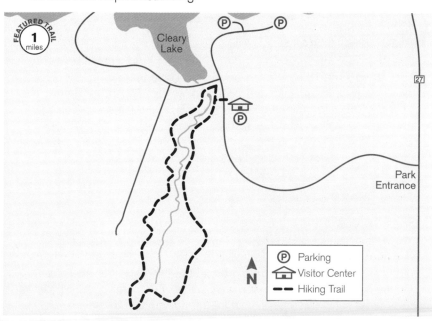

Coon Rapids Regional Dam

TOTAL TRAILS
4.2 miles

WHERE

On the Mississippi River, at the border of Coon Rapids and Brooklyn Park

DIRECTIONS

To reach Anoka County's East Visitor Center, take Interstate 35W north to County Road 10 NW. Continue straight onto Coon Rapids Boulevard NW, then turn left on Egret Boulevard NW to the park. To reach the Three Rivers Parks' West Visitor Center, take Highway 610 to the Noble Parkway exit; turn north on Noble; east on 97th Avenue; then north on County Road 12 (Russell Avenue) to the park.

OVERVIEW

The Mississippi and the impressive dam are the main attractions here. The "million dollar plant" was built in 1913 to provide electricity for streetcars running from Minneapolis to Anoka. The dam generated power until it closed in 1966. Three Rivers Parks operates the rebuilt dam, which makes recreational boating on the river possible.

RECOMMENDED TRAILS

The Anoka County trailhead is north of the east visitor center, near the boat launch. The Three Rivers trailhead is behind the west visitor center, along the river. Hikers can start in either Hennepin or Anoka County. The best river views along the trail are on the west side. Hikers can walk on the 1.7-mile Cottonwood Trail alongside islands and the tranquil back channel; this trail leads to the .8-mile Wood Duck Trail, a lovely, secluded stroll through forest bottomland and over two wooden footbridges.

TERRAIN

Almost all the trails are flat.

OTHER TRAILS

The Anoka County section has 1.7 miles of gravel trails plus an un-mapped wealth of smaller dirt trails worth exploring. Pick up the informal dirt trails just north of the picnic grills, where the gravel trail also starts. On the dam's west side, there are 2.5 miles of dirt, grass, and woodchip trails. Both parks also offer paved trails for hikers and bikers.

Park Highlight!

Nowhere else in the Twin Cities will you see the Mississippi River like this. Take a stroll across the impressive 1,000-foot dam and see the river as a potent force of nature as a wall of water rushes forth.

FACILITIES

bait/tackle
benches
bike/ski rentals
exhibits

pavilions
picnic area
restrooms

visitor centers
water fountains

COST

free

CONTACTS

East Visitor Center, 763-757-4700 or www.anokacountyparks.com and
West Visitor Center, 763-694-7790 or www.threeriversparkdistrict.org

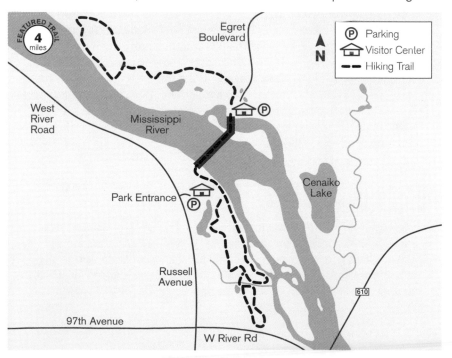

Cottage Grove Ravine Park

SURFACE: dirt, grass, woodchips

WHERE

Cottage Grove

DIRECTIONS

From Highway 61, take the County Road 19 (Innovation Road) exit.
Go north on 19 over the highway overpass and then turn right onto East
Point Douglas Road. Turn left into the park.

OVERVIEW

This Washington County park is small, but includes a neat four-mile loop
through a two-mile-long ravine. Located just off of Highway 61 by a
drive-in movie theater, this urban park still ends up feeling fairly woodsy.

RECOMMENDED TRAILS

From the park entrance, bear right at the fork in the road and drive half a
mile to the picnic area. The trailhead is just right of the picnic shelter. It's
easy to follow the trail, which is marked with numbers. From the picnic
shelter trailhead, hikers will begin climbing up the trail and continue going
uphill until reaching the open meadow at the north end of the park. From
there, hikers can walk down and up a few more hills back to the trailhead.
The trails feature healthy woods, and the park is known for its wildlife,
especially birds. Watch for Pileated Woodpeckers, Louisiana Waterthrush
and other warblers in this park.

TERRAIN

Not surprisingly, this ravine park features a good number of rolling hills.

OTHER TRAILS

The wide, well-marked trails made of dirt, grass, and woodchips range
past numerous oaks, pines, and aspens. In winter, these trails are ski-only.
The dirt trails here don't all connect, so to reach all of them hikers need
to briefly walk along some paved paths or through the parking lot. There's
another smaller trailhead closer to the park entrance for a .7-mile trail.

Park Highlight!

It's easy to forget you're near a busy highway in this park. The wide, comfortable trails here are a must-see for those in the east metro and include the park's namesake, a two-mile-long ravine.

FACILITIES

bathrooms

benches

grills

picnic shelters

playground

water

COST

Parking pass required. Washington County permits are also good at Anoka and Carver County parks.

CONTACTS

Contact Washington County Parks 651-430-8370, or www.co.washington.mn.us

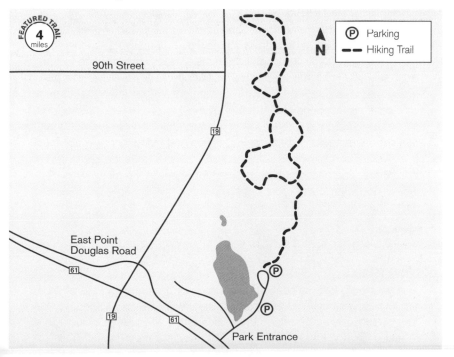

Crosby Farm Regional Park

SURFACE: paved

WHERE

St. Paul

DIRECTIONS

From Highway 35E, take the Shepard Road exit and head west 2 miles. Turn left at Gannon Road/Crosby Farm Road and drive half a mile to the main entrance at the park's west end. Crosby's east entrance near the 35E bridge has parking for three or four cars.

OVERVIEW

Tens of thousands of people visit this city park each year, strolling past some of the 300 plant species here, which include a colony of Kentucky coffee trees, a rare, native Minnesota tree.

RECOMMENDED TRAILS

Hikers can pick up the trails just behind the stone picnic shelter. Crosby's roughly three miles of main trails are paved and mostly flat and its forest floodplain, lakes, and wetlands border the Mississippi River and include good views of the confluence with the Minnesota River. When the paved trail curves away from the river, hikers can opt to follow the trail through oak woods or continue straight along skinny dirt side trails that hug the Mississippi shoreline. The trails along Upper Lake curve past wetlands and sedge meadows. Come spring, ephemeral plants sprinkle the forest floor with color. By summer, the park's lakes and wetlands seem covered in lily pads. The river and lakes here attract herons, egrets, barred owls, belted kingfishers, and other birds and waterfowl. In winter, eagles feed along the river.

TERRAIN

The river floodplain is fairly flat.

OTHER TRAILS

The trails from Crosby continue west and north to Hidden Falls and east to Lilydale Regional Park. Ambitious hikers who want a daylong adventure could explore trails along both sides of the Mississippi including Lilydale, Crosby, Hidden Falls, Fort Snelling, and the Winchell Trails.

FACILITIES

grills
fire pit
fishing pier
picnic shelter

Park Highlight!

Come here for the fabulous, up-close views of the Mississippi River and the many birds and waterfowl that live and fly along the waterway.

restrooms
vending machine (nearby) | water fountain

COST

free

CONTACTS

St. Paul Parks and Recreation, 651-632-5111 or www.ci.stpaul.mn.us

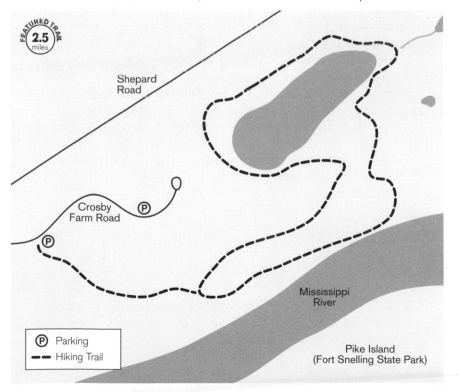

Crow-Hassan Park Reserve

SURFACE: dirt, grass, sand, gravel

WHERE

Rogers

DIRECTIONS

From Interstate 94, go north to the Rogers exit, then south through Rogers. Turn right on County Road 116, (Territorial Road), and go to County Road 203 (Sylvan Lake Road). Turn left and continue on 203 to the park entrance.

OVERVIEW

Miles of tall grasses ripple along rolling hills, past lakes, wetlands, the river, and some 600 acres of restored prairie.

RECOMMENDED TRAILS

The hike-only trailhead is at the south side of the parking lot. The trails are mostly ruts of dirt, grass, sand, or gravel surrounded by tall grasses. Hikers may want long pants here to protect their legs from the park's many insects and tall grasses. The trail winds past great swaths of grasslands in shades of green, blue, red, and copper, interspersed with trees and shrubs. In spring, wildflowers paint the rolling hillsides purple. Sumac, oaks, and aspen are common here, as are hawks, eagles, fox and coyotes. To complete the hiking trail loop, hikers need to walk along horse-hike trails of soft sand and lumpy gravel dented with hoof prints. This western section of horse trail overlooks the muddy Crow River.

TERRAIN

A number of rolling hills, including a few somewhat steep hills along the horse trails.

OTHER TRAILS

Most of Crow-Hassan's 17.6 miles of hiking trails are shared with horses and dogs. The horse-hike trailhead is at the north side of the parking lot. From the hike-horse trailhead, hikers can head north along the wide sand, gravel, and grass trail past a savanna.

FACILITIES

camping
canoe launch | picnic tables
off-leash dog area | vault toilets | water fountains

COST

free

CONTACTS

Three Rivers Park District, 763-694-7860 or www.threeriversparks.org

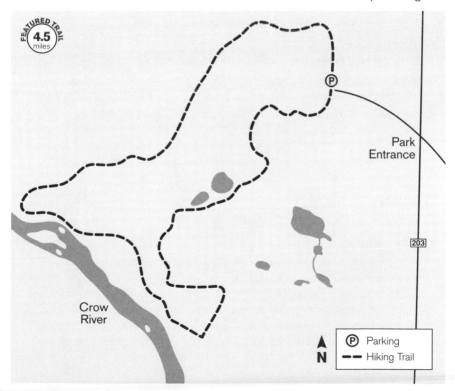

Elm Creek Regional Park

SURFACE: grass, dirt, paved

WHERE
Maple Grove

DIRECTIONS
From Interstate 94, take County Road 81 north, then turn right at Elm Creek Blvd. Take the second right and follow signs to the park. To reach Eastman Nature Center, stay on County Road 81 until Fernbrook Lane/County Road 121. Turn right, then turn right onto Elm Creek Road. Turn right at the entrance to the nature center.

OVERVIEW
The largest of the Three Rivers District's parks, Elm Creek's 5,000-plus acres span endless miles of trails along rolling grasslands, reconstructed prairies, lakes, and woods.

RECOMMENDED TRAILS
The scenic trails around Eastman Nature Center are an ideal spot to start. Hikers can wander 3.5 miles through four easy loops, which are open year-round. Eastman's sugar maples and big basswoods give way to the more open meadows along the Monarch Trail. From there, hikers can continue onto the Creek Trail, which winds by Rush Creek. The lovely trails pass through woods and recreated prairies, and cross bridges over creeks and wetlands.

TERRAIN
Many rolling hills but almost no steep climbs.

OTHER TRAILS
This sprawling park has seven trailheads. About half of Elm Creek's fifty-plus miles of hiking trails are paved, and many of the unpaved grass and dirt trails are shared. But the trails are quite wide, so there's room for everyone. The nature center trails are closed at 3:30 p.m. on weekends for the deer watch program. The Thicket, Valley, and Northern Lights trails at the park's south end are lit for skiers in winter and for hikers in spring and fall.

FACILITIES

- archery range
- beach
- cafeteria
- camping
- exhibits
- off-leash dog area

- nature center
- phones
- winter sports rentals

- restrooms
- visitor center

COST

free

CONTACTS

Eastman Nature Center, 763-694-7700; Visitor Center, 763-694-7894 or www.threeriversparkdistrict.org

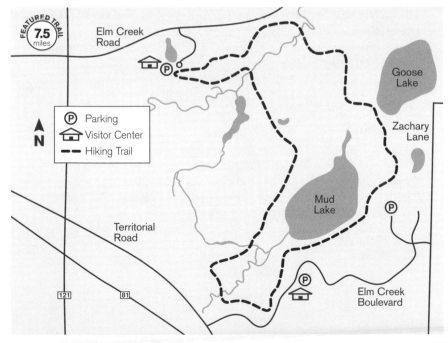

SURFACE: dirt, woodchip

WHERE

Minneapolis

DIRECTIONS

From Highway 55, take Theodore Wirth Parkway south .5 mile, then turn left at the entrance to the wildflower garden. Proceed up the hill to the meter-only parking area.

OVERVIEW

Established in 1907 by the Minneapolis botany teacher for whom it is named, the wildflower garden was once a tamarack bog and is now part of Minneapolis's biggest park, the 743-acre Theodore Wirth Park. The garden is open seasonally, from April 1 to October 15, 7:30 a.m. to dusk.

RECOMMENDED TRAILS

The gated entrance to the garden is just north of the parking lot. The garden's compact fifteen acres encompass woodland, wetland, and prairie. Numbered posts identify plants and trees described in a terrific booklet sold in the shelter.

TERRAIN

Gentle hills with one fairly steep rise.

OTHER TRAILS

From the wetlands, hikers can climb a steep hill to highest point in the garden, the prairie. Although the garden's trails are less than a mile long, they include numerous benches and seasonal water fountains. Wirth Park's Quaking Bog, just south of the wildflower garden, also is worth hiking, especially the floating boardwalk.

FACILITIES

| bathrooms | exhibits | small store |
| benches | shelters | |

Park Highlight!

Planted in the shadow of downtown Minneapolis, this gem of a garden lets urban dwellers savor natural beauty and wildlife.

COST

Bring change for
parking meters;
$5 for plant and tree booklet

CONTACTS

Eloise Butler Wildflower Garden 612-370-4903, or
http://www.minneapolisparks.org

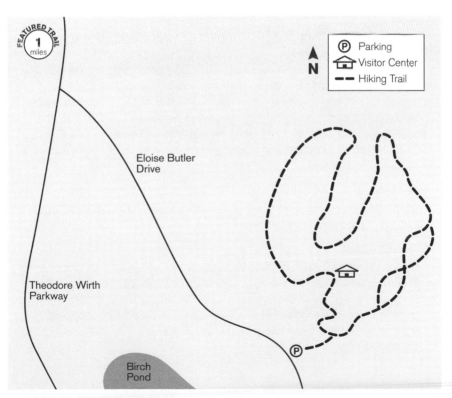

Fort Snelling State Park

SURFACE: dirt, gravel, paved

WHERE
Minneapolis

DIRECTIONS
From Highway 5, take the Post Road exit and head east. Drive down a steep hill into the park. Park in the visitor center parking lot.

OVERVIEW
This is an urban park. Airplanes thunder overhead, cars buzz along nearby highways, and homes and buildings are visible just across the river. Still, this pleasant park draws many visitors, including dog walkers, day hikers, picnickers, beachgoers, anglers, and skiers.

RECOMMENDED TRAILS
Fort Snelling's best hiking is on Pike Island, a slender swath of land sandwiched between the Mississippi and Minnesota rivers. From the trailhead, head east on a paved path that leads to a footbridge to the island. Bikes aren't allowed on the island. Native Americans consider the land sacred; settlers and soldiers saw value here also. Lt. Zebulon Pike camped here during his 1805 western expedition. The army built Fort Snelling, which overlooks the island and confluence, to control the area's trade and settlement.

TERRAIN
One steep paved hill up to the fort, but otherwise, Snelling's trails, especially on Pike Island, are fairly flat.

OTHER TRAILS
Fort Snelling's 18 miles of trails are easy walking—mostly flat and wide. The main trailhead is by the visitor center, but other trails begin across from the park office and also east of the Minnesota River, behind the Sibley House in Mendota. Hikers who finish the Pike Island loop and want to walk more can explore other trails in the park or climb a sharp paved trail to the fort.

Park Highlight!

Hike on Pike Island for a wonderful view of two of our state's biggest rivers, the Mississippi and the Minnesota.

FACILITIES

- beach
- boat ramp
- exhibits
- fishing pier
- picnic sites
- playground
- restrooms
- visitor center
- water fountains

COST

state park permit required

CONTACT

Fort Snelling State Park, 612-725-2389 or
www.dnr.state.mn.us/state parks

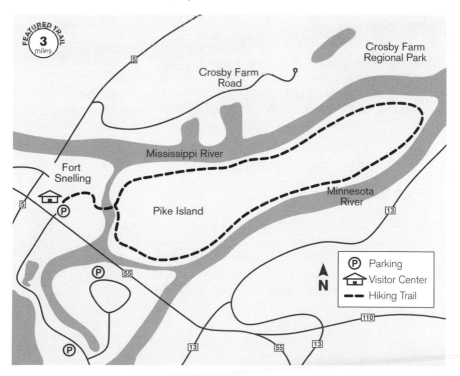

Hyland Lake Park Reserve

SURFACE: paved, dirt, woodchip

WHERE

Bloomington

DIRECTIONS

From Highway 494, go south on East Bush Lake Road. At the stoplight, turn right and follow East Bush Lake Road, which veers right. Continue for about one mile, then turn left at the entrance to Richardson Nature Center. The entrance to the visitor center and play area is another mile south on East Bush Lake Road.

OVERVIEW

People and waterfowl flock to this park, which is rich with woodlands, lakes, ponds, and restored prairie.

RECOMMENDED TRAILS

There are two main trailheads, one at the park's north end, one at the south end. The trails at the park's northern end are less than a mile each and offer varied views of woods, water, and grassland. Here, hikers can wander north by the Turtle Basking Pond and restored tallgrass prairie and then pick up the wooded Oak Trail, which includes a viewing station. The pretty Aspen and Muskrat trails bring hikers back to the nature center.

TERRAIN

Two big hills for skiers, with several tamer hills scattered throughout.

OTHER TRAILS

About half of Hyland's 20 miles of hiking trails are paved; all trails here are wide, smooth, and easy to walk. Hikers who want a longer walk can head south from the nature center on the open Osprey Trail. From there, hikers can walk the two-mile North Trail loop as well as the shrubby Oak Knob Trail that leads to the visitor center. From the visitor center, hikers can explore the Lake Trail, which winds south around Hyland Lake.

FACILITIES

concessions
disc golf
driving range
equip. rentals
exhibits

nature center
playground
restrooms

vending machines
water fountains

COST

free

CONTACT

Richardson Nature Center, 763-694-7676; Visitor Center, 763-694-7687, or www.threeriversparkdistrict.org

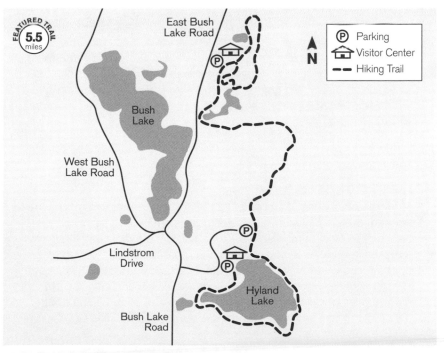

Lake Elmo Park Reserve

SURFACE: dirt, grass, gravel

WHERE

Lake Elmo

DIRECTIONS

From Interstate 94, take County Road 19 north to County Road 10. Cross County Road 10 and proceed into the park. There are multiple parking areas.

OVERVIEW

Two large lakes frame this park's rolling hills of forests and prairies, luring anglers, equestrians, mountain bikers, hikers, and skiers.

RECOMMENDED TRAILS

The ski trail parking lot, located about .5 mile north of the park office, is also the trailhead for the turf hiking trails. The park's six miles of hike-only trails—Loops B and C—are east of the park road. Multi-use Loop A, west of the park road, offers excellent views of the herons and other waterfowl around Eagle Point Lake. Along the more wooded southwest side of Loop A, hikers can visit a large ski shelter with a wood-burning stove, picnic tables, and chairs. Although the trails west of the park road are shared with horses and bikes, they are wide enough to accommodate all who visit this rolling 2,165-acre park.

TERRAIN

Many gently rolling hills.

OTHER TRAILS

Many of Lake Elmo's 20 miles of dirt, grass, and gravel hiking trails are open to hikers, mountain bikers, and horses. The park's six miles of hike-only trails—Loops B and C—are east of the park road. Hikers who walk all of Loops A, B, and C will end up passing all kinds of campsites. Loops A and C have shortcuts so hikers can avoid the camps, but Loop B goes right past modern campgrounds for recreational vehicles. If that's not your idea of hiking, skip Loop B, which is 3.1 miles. Along Loop C, the sounds of gunshots may punctuate the air; the Oakdale Gun Club is about 200 yards east of the park.

Park Highlight!

Loop around picturesque Eagle Point Lake and see the beach and the lake's many waterfowl and pretty cattails.

FACILITIES

archery range
beach
boat launch
fishing pier

equestrian camp
orienteering course
playgrounds

restrooms
water fountains

COST

Washington County Park permit required

CONTACT

Lake Elmo Park Reserve, 651-430-8370 or www.co.washington.mn.us

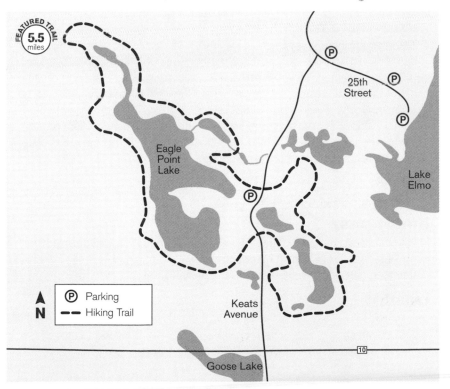

Lake Rebecca Park Reserve

SURFACE: dirt, grass, paved

WHERE

Independence

DIRECTIONS

From Highway 55, go west to County Road 50. Turn left and follow to the park entrance.

OVERVIEW

Big swans and Big Woods grace this sprawling park of lakes, wetlands, savannas, and woods. In sections of the park, stands of tall maple and basswood trees stretch to the sky creating a green canopy with an airy, open forest floor.

RECOMMENDED TRAILS

The main trailhead is by the Hilltop shelter. During construction, the park has a temporary hike-dog trailhead farther east on County Road 50. The 3.5-mile hike-mountain bike trail passes a lovely overlook with information about trumpeter swans, which can be spotted in the area. The hike-horse trails are wider, and in some cases, fairly rough, but include a wonderful section of Big Woods along the park's southern boundary. Rolling grass-lands, interspersed with healthy pines, offer good views of Lake Rebecca and the park's other lakes and marshes.

TERRAIN

A good number of rolling hills.

OTHER TRAILS

Hikers share almost all of the 21 miles of dirt and grass turf trails with horses, dogs, or mountain bikes. Hikers who want a longer walk can tour the perimeter on nine miles of shared turf trails.

FACILITIES

beach	camping	playground
boat launch	fishing pier	vault toilets
boat rentals	picnic shelters	water fountains

COST
free

CONTACT
Lake Rebecca Park Reserve, 763-694-7860 or www.threeriversparks.org

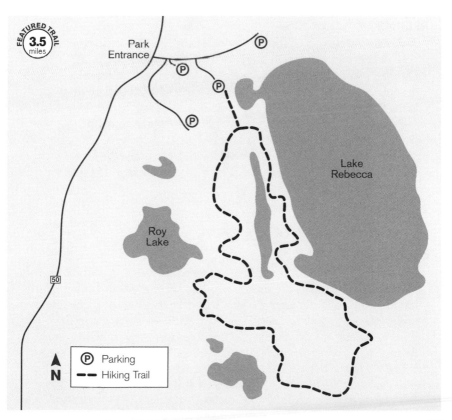

FEATURED TRAIL
3.5 miles

Park Entrance

Lake Rebecca

Roy Lake

50

P Parking
- - Hiking Trail

N

Lebanon Hills Regional Park

SURFACE: dirt, grass, gravel

WHERE
Eagan and Apple Valley

DIRECTIONS
From Highway 35E, take Cliff Road east to the main park entrance. Turn right and continue to the beach and visitor center parking area.

OVERVIEW
Dakota County's biggest park boasts 2,000 acres of woods and lakes that suit hikers, paddlers, mountain bikers, equestrians, and anglers.

RECOMMENDED TRAILS
The main trailhead is by the visitor center and Schulze Lake beach. From here, hikers can walk north away from the beach toward the .83-mile Discovery Trail. Frequent signs tell quick facts about the trees, trails, and animals here. The Discovery Trail starts alongside Schulze Lake, then loops through a woodland of elm, oak, box elder and aspen. This short trail leads to the longer Voyageur Trail that stretches west around Lake Jensen and is particularly scenic. Narrow dirt trails hug the shoreline past silver maples and box elders. In season, lily pads adorn the lake. Ducks, pheasants, hawks, and many other birds take advantage of Lebanon Hills' rich, aquatic landscape.

TERRAIN
Plenty of hills, some rolling, a few steep.

OTHER TRAILS
Lebanon Hill's 14 miles of dirt, gravel, and grass trails curl past lakes, marshes, and rolling hills. Lebanon Hills has five trailheads, three of which are for hikers; and one each for horses and mountain bikes. The mountain bike trailhead on Johnny Cake Ridge Road includes some hiking trails. Hikers who want to continue west past Lake Jensen can walk several more miles of trails, mostly through pine forests. Farther west, at the mountain bike trailhead on Johnny Cake Ridge Road, are two more loops of hiking trails that skirt the bike trails. The trails east of Schulze Lake pass through fine stands of red pines and along cattail-lined edges of Marsh Lake.

FACILITIES

bathrooms
beach
camping
fishing gear

phone
picnic shelters
rentals

retreat center
visitor center

COST

free

CONTACT

Lebanon Hills Regional Park visitor center 651-554-6530 or
www.co.dakota.mn.us

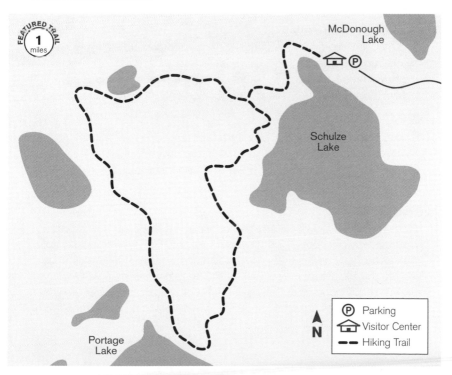

Lilydale Regional Park

SURFACE: dirt, gravel, lumpy bricks

WHERE

St. Paul

DIRECTIONS

From Highway 35E, take exit 102 onto eastbound Highway 13. Just past the 35E overpass, take an immediate right onto Lilydale Road. Continue on Lilydale into the park's gravel parking lot.

OVERVIEW

Stashed just south of Mississippi River near downtown St. Paul, Lilydale beckons fossil hunters, ice climbers, and adventurers. For almost a century, the Twin Cities Brick Company mined this St. Paul river bluff for its clay. The extensive digging revealed countless fossils.

RECOMMENDED TRAILS

The main trailhead is by the park's fossil ground parking lot. From here, hikers can head west along a wide gravel trail. Where the trail begins climbing toward the East Clay Pit, hikers can take a brief detour to check out an old brick oven and cave. The city has sealed entrances to these caves.

TERRAIN

Carved into the river bluffs, Lilydale's trails are steep and demanding. Hikers who prefer flat trails should walk the paved trail along the river or opt for the Cherokee Heights Drive trailheads and take the short trail to the scenic overlook.

OTHER TRAILS

From the East Clay Pit, hikers can continue up the main trail and explore several offshoots. Countless side trails cut through the park, but it's easy to stay on the main wide gravel and dirt trail. Other side trails lead to the Middle and West Clay pits. Those pits are near wetlands, so expect soggy boots. But the views of the old brick mining pits are great. Lilydale's Pickerel Lake has an active eagle nest and also attracts herons and blue-winged teal.

Park Highlight!

Head to Lilydale for great views of the river, and check out the former brickyard where you can find old bricks and even older seashells and fossils.

FACILITIES

boat launch
fossil hunting
ice climbing
water, picnic area, and restrooms at nearby
Harriet Island Regional Park (1 mile east)

COST

Permit required for fossil hunters and ice climbers

CONTACT

City of St. Paul Parks and Rec, 651-266-6400, or
www.ci.stpaul.mn.us/parks. For fossil hunting or ice climbing permits,
651-832-5111. The National Park Service also has information and
maps about Lilydale at www.nps.gov/miss

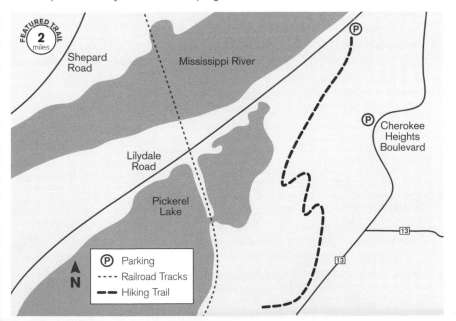

Long Lake Regional Park

SURFACE: dirt, paved

WHERE

New Brighton

DIRECTIONS

From Interstate 35W, take the County Road 96 exit. Go west one block on 96, then turn left and head south on Old Highway 8 NW and turn right into the park entrance. Continue driving into the park to the parking area by the New Brighton History Center.

OVERVIEW

This Ramsey County park preserves the area's past; today, many people come to the park for its lake attractions—a swimming beach, boat launch, and fishing pier.

RECOMMENDED TRAILS

From the parking area just northeast of the history center, hikers can begin walking on a small patch of restored prairie by Rush Lake. Just before the prairie path leads to the lake, it comes to a T. Hikers can opt to turn left and go north into woods at the park's north end. Or hikers can choose to turn right and head south on wider, more developed trails through the middle of the park. From a car, the natural landscape doesn't look like much, but up close, hikers can savor the many wildflowers and lilting birdsong. The Rush Lake dirt trails end and hikers can opt to head north back to the history center parking lot or begin walking the paved trails through the park.

TERRAIN

Easy, mostly mild and flat trails.

OTHER TRAILS

This 225-acre park has three miles of wide paved trails that are shared with bikes, as well as dirt trails that loop through tangled woods and open prairie. The southernmost mile of paved trail, along Long Lake, is noisy due to nearby Highway 694, but that section is worth walking for the interpretative signs. Hikers can also pick up the paved trails from the history center.

FACILITIES

beach
bathrooms
boat launch
concessions

fishing pier
history center
pavilion

playground
water (seasonal)

COST

free

CONTACT

Ramsey County Parks and Recreation, 651-748-2500 or
www.co.ramsey.mn.us/parks.

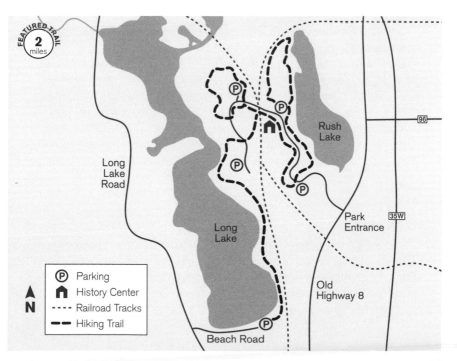

Maplewood Nature Center

SURFACE: dirt, gravel, boardwalk

WHERE

Maplewood

DIRECTIONS

From Interstate 94, go north on Century Avenue/MN-120. One block past Minnehaha Avenue turn left and go west on East 7th Street to the nature center parking lot.

OVERVIEW

Green herons, geese, ducks, turtles, and other water dwellers are easy to spot at this suburban park set around a scenic pond. *The Twin Cities Birding Map* notes this park has resident Great Horned Owls.

RECOMMENDED TRAILS

The main trailhead is by the nature center. The Green Heron Trail loop is almost a mile and easy to walk, with a relatively level dirt and crushed gravel path. The trail loops around the pond, which is actually a shallow marsh. Most of this path and the entire boardwalk are wheelchair accessible. Biking, dog-walking, running, jogging, skiing and skating are prohibited here. At the end of the south end of the trail there is a 620-foot boardwalk. The west side of the trail includes a pretty loop through woods and water. Oaks, shrubs and silver maples thrive here. The westernmost interpretative point highlights a gorgeous silver maple. The trail's south side passes a slender swath of prairie.

TERRAIN

Flat and level.

OTHER TRAILS

Three smaller trailheads offer access to the surrounding neighborhoods. The city of Maplewood also has several neighborhood preserves. Joy Park, for example, is five miles north of the nature center. Some of the neighborhood preserves have trails but none offer amenities.

FACILITIES

benches
exhibits
nature center
observation deck
rentals

restrooms
water
water garden

COST

free

CONTACT

Maplewood Nature Center (closed on Sundays and Mondays),
651-249-2170 or www.ci.maplewood.mn.us/nc

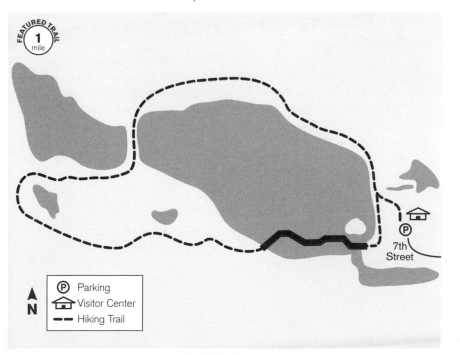

FEATURED TRAIL
1 mile

P Parking
🏠 Visitor Center
–– Hiking Trail

7th Street

N

Minnehaha Park

SURFACE: dirt, paved, boardwalk

WHERE
Minneapolis

DIRECTIONS
From Highway 55 (Hiawatha Avenue), go east on 46th Street two blocks to Minnehaha Avenue. Turn right and go south on Minnehaha Avenue one block. At the roundabout, turn left and go east on Minnehaha Parkway to the pay parking lot.

OVERVIEW
Since 1889, when Minneapolis first acquired this parkland, Minnehaha has had a zoo, tourist camp, and a depot that once saw more than three dozen train trips a day. Minnehaha, which means "laughing waters," was the name Henry Wadsworth Longfellow bestowed on this waterfall in his poem "The Song of Hiawatha."

RECOMMENDED TRAILS
From the overlook by the waterfalls, paved trails loop through the park. Steep stone steps lead down to the base of the falls and to dirt trails that hug both sides of Minnehaha Creek to the Mississippi River. The trails on the east side of the creek are wider and flatter and the creekside trails, shaded by tall cottonwoods, oaks, maples, and basswood, offer close-up views of the park's limestone bluffs. Just before the river, hikers can head back to the falls or opt to climb 157 somewhat decrepit stone steps on the west side that lead up to Minnehaha Park's south end. It's worth exploring the park's paved trails above the falls.

OTHER TRAILS
For those looking for a little adventure, check out the trails on the west side of Minnehaha Creek. Here, dirt trails lead to a long boardwalk and then a rocky, rooty, tricky section of often muddy trail. Several bridges along the way allow hikers to cross the creek, which eventually flows into the Mississippi River.

FACILITIES

- bandstand
- grills
- off-leash dog area
- pavilion
- playground
- picnic tables
- restaurant
- restrooms
- surrey rentals
- water

COST

free

CONTACT

Minneapolis Park and Recreation Board, 612-230-6400 or www.minneapolispark.org

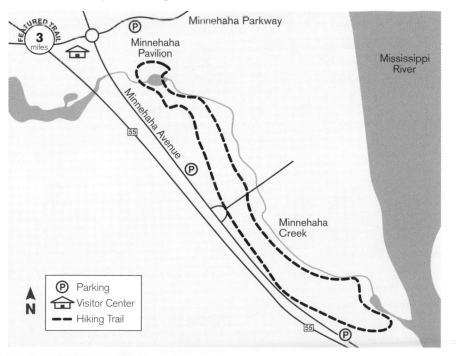

Murphy-Hanrehan Park Reserve

SURFACE: dirt, grass

WHERE

Savage

DIRECTIONS

From Interstate 35W, take County Road 42 west to County Road 27. Turn left and go south to 154th Street. Turn left and head east, then turn right onto County Road 75 (Murphy Lake Boulevard) to the park entrance. Park in the nearby lot.

OVERVIEW

This rustic 2,400-acre park attracts rare woodland songbirds along with many hikers, mountain bikers, and cross-country skiers who enjoy the heart-thumping hills. Unlike other Three Rivers parks, Murphy-Hanrehan doesn't have added amenities. The attraction here is the land itself.

RECOMMENDED TRAILS

The main trailhead for hiking and mountain biking is by County Road 75, at the park's north end. The shared bike-hike trails feature Murphy-Hanrehan's finest views. Some of the trails are only open to hikers from August to November because rare birds nest here. In fact, this area has Minnesota's only known nesting population of hooded warblers. Acadian flycatchers and blue-winged warblers also make their home here. The National Audubon Society considers this park an "Important Bird Area."

TERRAIN

Many, many hills. Hikers who relish hills should explore Murphy-Hanrehan's north trails. Hikers who prefer less rigorous climbs can roam Murphy's south trails or visit nearby Cleary Lake Regional Park, which features pleasant and mostly flat trails.

OTHER TRAILS

Murphy-Hanrehan includes more than twenty miles of hiking trails, with seven miles of hike-only trails. The rest are shared with horses, bikes, or dogs. The horse camp trailhead, which also has hiking trails, is on Sunset Lake Road, about three miles south of the County Road 75 trailhead.

FACILITIES

boat launch
phone
picnic shelter | vault toilets | water fountain

COST

free

CONTACT

For information about Murphy-Hanrehan, call Cleary Lake Regional Park, 763-694-7777 or visit www.threeriversparks.org

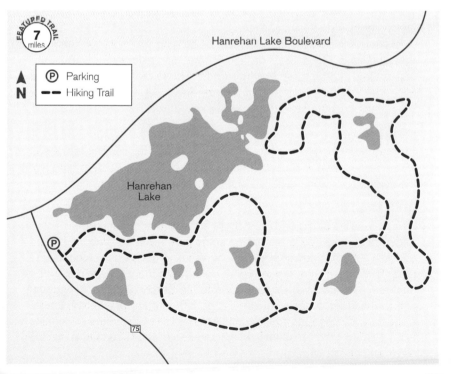

Richard T. Anderson Conservation Area

SURFACE: dirt, grass, gravel

WHERE

Eden Prairie

DIRECTIONS

From Highway 494, take Highway 212 (Flying Cloud Drive) west. Continue for 6.3 miles, then turn right into the park.

OVERVIEW

Named for an environmentalist city council member, the Richard T. Anderson Conservation Area features gorgeous trails, great views from bluffs and a wealth of informative signs.

RECOMMENDED TRAILS

The main trailhead is by the parking lot on Flying Cloud Drive. A smaller parking area is northeast of the main trailhead at Settler's Ridge. The west section is challenging and sublime, offering the most rewarding trails and views. A nonprofit group, Writers Rising Up, helped create the fact-packed interpretive trail that tells the story of writer Elizabeth Fries Ellet, the first white woman to visit here. She called this area a Garden of Eden, thus inspiring the city's name.

TERRAIN

Several challenging, steep hills. The westernmost trail, leading to the basswood-maple forest, is probably the toughest climb. The eastern trails along the oak savanna and prairie are steep but have more gradual inclines.

OTHER TRAILS

RTA's five miles of dirt and grass trails are well marked and offer marvelous hiking. Along the north central part of the trail, wooden steps end at a suburban subdivision. Hikers who skip the steps can continue east. That trail ends at a paved park road. From there, hikers can turn right and head south a few feet down to the Settler's Ridge parking area and trailhead. From there, hikers can go left onto the prairie trail, then along a sandy ridge top overlooking the river valley. From the ridge, hikers can walk down the grass trail, which parallels Flying Cloud Drive, back to the main parking lot.

FACILITIES

picnic tables
vault toilets
water fountain

COST

free

CONTACT

City of Eden Prairie Parks and Recreation Department, 952-949-8442
www.edenprairie.org, or www.writersrisingup.org.

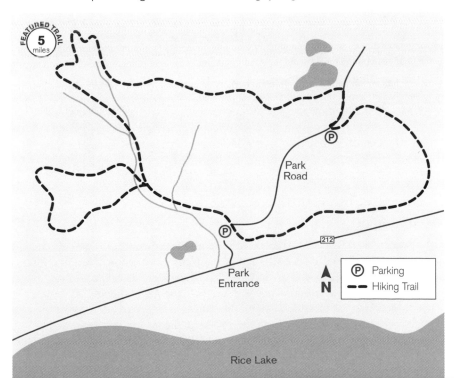

Spring Lake Park Reserve

SURFACE: dirt, grass, gravel

WHERE

Hastings

DIRECTIONS

From Highway 55 east, take County Road 42 east to Idell Avenue. Turn left and go north on Idell to the Schaar's Bluff archway. Turn right through the arch and continue into the parking area. To reach the park's lower area, take Highway 55 east to Pine Bend Trail. Head north on Pine Bend, then turn right and head north on Fahey Avenue. Turn right into the park.

OVERVIEW

Named for a lake that no longer exists, this panoramic park along the bluffs showcases the Mississippi River, which is a mile wide here.

RECOMMENDED TRAILS

The main trailhead is at Schaar's Bluff, by the visitor center. From here, hikers can walk along the paved path and check out the fabulous river views. A smaller trailhead for the park's lower area is off of Pine Bend Trail. Here, the river overlook is exceptional. The half-mile hiking trail to the river leads to a view of the Mississippi that seems more like the Boundary Waters.

TERRAIN

Some rolling hills, but mostly flat trails.

OTHER TRAILS

Schaar's Bluff has four miles of dirt, grass, and gravel trails. The 1.7 miles of mostly flat trails northeast of the picnic area range through pretty woods and over a beautiful stone bridge. The 1.9 miles south of the visitor center span rolling hills and curve past woods and fields. Hikers who don't like narrow trails, steps, or cliffside river views can opt for a alternate trail that cuts through the middle of the woods. From the visitor center, hikers can also cross a modern bridge that leads to the south Schaar Bluff trails. The wide trails here are hillier and offer few views of the river.

Park Highlight!

This park boasts phenomenal views of the Mississippi River's widest point. In spots here, it's impossible to see the far side of the river. No other Twin Cities park offers this picture of the Mississippi.

FACILITIES

archery range
bathrooms
model airfield
garden plots
picnic shelters

play area
retreat center
visitor center

water fountains

COST

free

CONTACT

Dakota County Parks, 952-891-7000 or www.co.dakota.mn.us

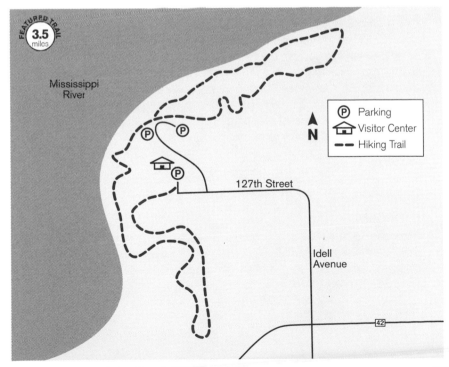

St. Croix Bluffs Regional Park

SURFACE: dirt, grass, gravel

WHERE

Hastings

DIRECTIONS

From Interstate 94, head south on State Highway 95, then turn left and head east on County Road 20. Just before Afton State Park, turn right and head south on County Road 21 (St. Croix Trail). Turn left into the park entrance and park by the picnic shelters.

OVERVIEW

This Washington County park wraps along 3,800 feet of St. Croix River shoreline.

RECOMMENDED TRAILS

The main hiking trails begin by the picnic shelters and are easy to pick up near the Hilltop shelter, or the volleyball and tennis courts. The 2.2-mile Loop B starts across from the Hilltop shelter and curves around the park road almost back to the office, then passes the park's maintenance sheds before ranging into wooded bluff land. It's worth hiking this wide grass-and-dirt trail for the gorgeous views of oaks, maples, and pines from junctions 5 to 6 and 7. That southeast section of the trail also includes a few steep hills and some views of nearby farm fields and homes.

TERRAIN

There are steep hills, especially near the boat launch, the ravines, and bluffs. Steep stairs lead from the beach toward the picnic shelters.

OTHER TRAILS

From the Birch Hollow and Eagle Ridge volleyball courts, hikers can head down a gravel-and-dirt trail. Here, hikers pass several lovely wooden foot bridges, cedars, and oaks down to the beach, a slender crescent of sand lined with big rocks.

FACILITIES

beach
boat launch
conference center
playgrounds
restrooms

shelters
tennis court
vending machine

water fountains

COST

Washington County Park permit required

CONTACT

St. Croix Bluffs Regional Park, 651-430-8240 or
www.co.washington.mn.us

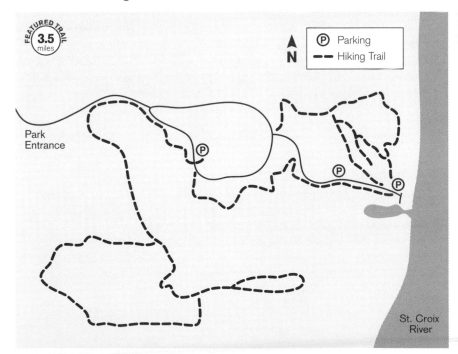

Tamarack Nature Center

SURFACE: dirt, grass, gravel, boardwalk

WHERE
White Bear Township

DIRECTIONS
From Highway 35E, take Highway 96 east to Otter Lake Road. Turn left and head north on Otter Lake Road, then turn left into the nature center parking lot.

OVERVIEW
Part of Bald Eagle-Otter Lake Regional Park, this Ramsey County nature preserve offers views of woods, wetlands, and prairie plus a lively assortment of wildlife.

RECOMMENDED TRAILS
It's easiest to start by the Children's Garden, just north of the nature center. The 1.3-mile Tamarack-Oak trails, which loop around Tamarack Lake's wetlands and woods, avoid views of the nearby highway and water tower and feature fun boardwalks of weathered wood over a shrub swamp. Depending on the season, hikers may get to see wildflowers like marsh marigolds. In any season, the Oak Trail is lovely.

TERRAIN
Mostly rolling hills, with a few more moderate inclines along the Fish Lake Trail on the park's west side.

OTHER TRAILS
Most of the center's four-plus miles of trails are grass, dirt, and boardwalk; they are lovely, but the sounds of traffic from nearby 35E are omnipresent. At trail post #7, hikers can opt to continue onto the 2.5 mile Goldenrod/ Fish Lake trails around a restored marsh and the preserve's perimeter. Hikers can finish their walk in two ways, on the Instructional Loop, a dirt trail circling a small field, or on the .5 mile paved Prairie Loop.

FACILITIES

exhibits
nature center
restrooms   snacks/pop
ski rentals   water fountain
(future plans include a pottery shed, an orchard, and play stream)

COST

free, as is a terrific booklet, *A Guide to Ramsey County Birding*, available in the nature center

CONTACT

Tamarack Nature Center, 651-407-5350 or
www.co.ramsey.mn.us/parks/

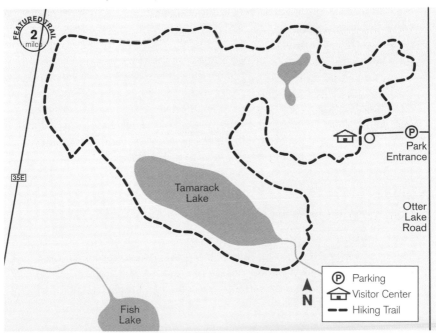

William O'Brien State Park

SURFACE: dirt, grass, gravel, boardwalk

WHERE

Marine on St. Croix

DIRECTIONS

From Interstate 94, take the Highway 95 North exit. Continue north for 21 miles then turn left into the park.

OVERVIEW

This varied 1,650-acre park gives visitors a chance to explore sloping savannas, dry prairies, sheltered woods, as well as a scenic river, wetlands, and lakes. Named for the logger who bought this land, this park protects some white pines, which once flourished here at Minnesota's oldest logging settlement but were cut almost to extinction.

RECOMMENDED TRAILS

Most of the hiking trails start behind the visitor center. From here, hikers can head north to walk the flat Wetland Trail, with massive stands of cattails and the chirps and chatter of aquatic creatures. A tunnel under train tracks leads to the Woodland Edge and the Hardwood Hills Trails, replete with basswood, cherry, ironwood, and ash trees. As the trail heads south, hikers can choose to do two side loops. The 1.1-mile Rolling Hills Savanna Trail swoops up and down past ponds, grasslands, and burly oaks. The adjacent Prairie Overlook Trail, climbs past a marsh into an upland prairie draped in big and little bluestem and wildflowers. Hikers cross train tracks to reach the Wedge Hill Savanna Trail which features a horizon-full of wetlands and loops back to the visitor center.

TERRAIN

Many rolling hills make this park fun to hike and a delight for skiers.

OTHER TRAILS

The twelve miles of wide dirt, grass, and gravel hiking trails roam over rolling hills and through woods, meadows, and forest floodplain. About a mile east of the visitor center, the Riverside Trail trundles past the St. Croix River and Lake Alice.

FACILITIES

boat launch
camping
exhibits
fishing areas
gift shop

equip. rental
restrooms
visitor center

water fountains

COST

state park permit required

CONTACT

William O'Brien State Park, 651-433-0500 or www.dnr.state.mn.us

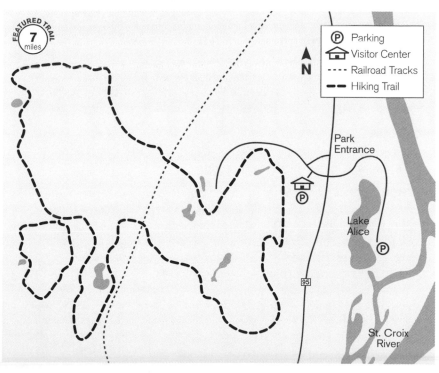

SURFACE: paved, dirt

WHERE
Minneapolis

DIRECTIONS
From Highway 55 (Hiawatha Avenue), head east on East 38th Street to Edmund Boulevard. Turn right and go south on West River Parkway to the 44th Street parking area.

OVERVIEW
Named for a prominent Minnesota geologist, this popular trail follows what was once a Dakota footpath along the Mississippi's only gorge. Some 10,000 years ago, an epic waterfall roared through this area, wearing away the sandstone and limestone rock walls. The waterfall receded, leaving behind the only gorge in the river's 2,350 miles.

RECOMMENDED TRAILS
From the 44th Street trailhead, hikers can enjoy fine views of the river-front and gorge, the bluffs across the river in St. Paul, and some of the many birds that migrate along this flyway. By the 36th Street trailhead, hikers will pass a small restored oak savanna nicknamed Giggly Hills.

TERRAIN
A few moderately steep hills and some steps leading up and down from the river and the restored oak savanna.

OTHER TRAILS
At a few points, the trail briefly ends. Hikers can walk along the paved path to reach the next Winchell Trail segment. From the 34th Street trail-head to 27th Street, the trail wanders along the sandy forest floodplain and continues under the Lake Street Bridge. After another brief trail break by a railroad bridge, hikers can continue north on dirt trails. Some sections of the trail here are closed to restore eroded areas. Just south of the Franklin Avenue Bridge, the trail ends, but the paved path along West River Parkway continues. A boulder by the bridge tells more about Newton Horace Winchell. In all, the trail stretches from the Franklin Avenue Bridge south to 44th street along West River Parkway.

Park Highlight!

This well-used trail overlooks the Mississippi River's only gorge and features great views of the river, bluffs, and many trees.

FACILITIES

vault toilet
water fountain

COST

free

CONTACT

Minneapolis Park Board, 612-230-6400 or www.minneapolisparks.org.
Also visit www.geo.umn.edu/Winchell_Trail.html and
www.nps.gov/miss/planyourvisit/seg12.htm

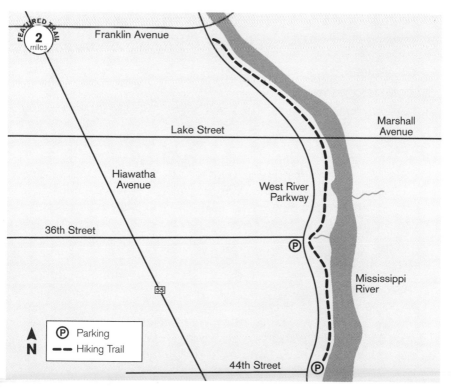

Wolsfeld Woods Scientific and Natural Area

SURFACE: dirt

WHERE
Orono

DIRECTIONS
From Highway 12, take Brown Road north .5 mile to County Road 6. Park in the Trinity Lutheran Church parking lot.

OVERVIEW
Thanks to maple syrup, this glorious patch of the Big Woods still stands in the Twin Cities and includes some of Minnesota's biggest sugar maples and the largest bitternut hickory tree. When this land was settled, the trees were tapped for maple syrup instead of being cleared for fields. Wolsfeld Woods is one of Minnesota's Scientific and Natural Areas, which means the land is open to public use but is kept in a primitive condition to preserve this sensitive resource. Visitors are required to stay on the marked trails.

RECOMMENDED TRAILS
Wolsfeld is divided into four areas, Areas A, B, C, and D. By the east side of the church parking lot, the main trailhead is marked by a big wooden sign and a posted map. From here, hikers can head east and south to wander through Area A and woods full of tall, straight-trunked trees. At a few creek crossings, hikers need to maneuver across casual bridges composed of haphazard logs and planks. The rough-hewn bridges and log steps melting into the trail are part of the charm of this primitive Scientific and Natural Area.

TERRAIN
Gently rolling hills.

OTHER TRAILS
Area B, in the wood's northwest section, overlooks Wolsfeld Lake and marshes bordering private property. This section can be soggy and is more open than the rest of Wolsfeld Woods. Areas C and D include mature red oaks, trout lily, toothwort, and false rue anemone. Wild mushrooms are prevalent here as well.

FACILITIES

COST

free

CONTACT

The Department of Natural Resources SNA Program 651-296-2855 or www.dnr.state.mn.us/snas

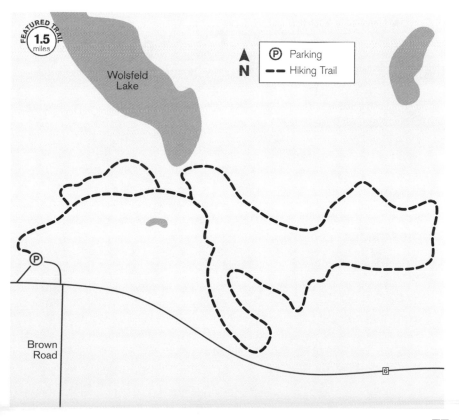

Wood Lake Nature Center

SURFACE: crushed gravel, boardwalk

WHERE

Richfield

DIRECTIONS

From 494, take the Lyndale Avenue exit and go north on Lyndale. Turn (west) on Lake Shore Drive then left again into the parking lot.

OVERVIEW

This "marsh in the middle of the city" gives urban dwellers a chance to experience nature without going far.

RECOMMENDED TRAILS

The trail starts by the nature center. Wood Lake feels and sounds urban; the park's west side borders Interstate 35W, but hikers who start out heading west can complete their walk on quieter trails. The Woodland Loop to the northwest is a quick treat of gorgeous cottonwood trees that seem to reach the clouds. Many places along the wide 1.8-mile Perimeter Trail feature good vistas of the big marsh as well as tall silver maples, box elders, and cottonwoods. The .8-mile Boardwalk Trail gives hikers a close-up look at Wood Lake's impressive marsh, where geese, ducks, red-winged blackbirds, and many other birds flock.

TERRAIN

Flat and level.

OTHER TRAILS

The three miles of crushed gravel trails and wood boardwalks are level and wheelchair-accessible during the summer. Hikers who like open areas can walk the .5 mile Prairie Trail, which traverses the marsh and a peaceful field of tall grasses. The trails along the park's east side include more understory shrubs and shorter trees such as red mulberry. Near the Forest Loop, hikers will pass a small observation deck that gives hikers another chance to gaze across the sweeping stretch of marshland flourishing amid the city.

FACILITIES

benches
exhibits
picnic tables

restrooms
visitor center

water fountain

COST

free

CONTACT

Wood Lake Nature Center, 612-861-9365 or
www.woodlakenaturecenter.org

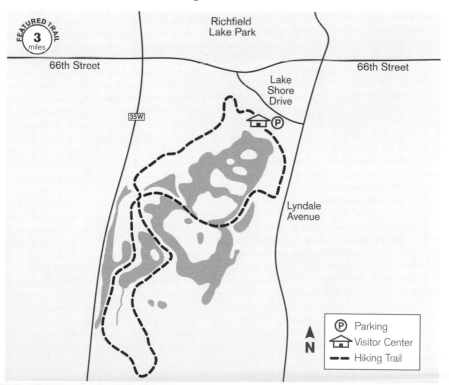

RESOURCES

Some hikers like to travel light and don't want to carry anything extra while out walking. Others don't mind stashing a small book or two in their packs to help them identify what they find out on the trails.

Below are details about the materials I used to learn about what's out on the trail.

Havelin, Kate, *Minnesota Running Trails: Dirt, Gravel, Rocks, and Roots*, Cambridge: Adventure Publications, 2006.

Kavanagh, James, *Minnesota Trees & Wildflowers: An Introduction to Familiar Species, Pocket Naturalist*, Phoenix: Waterford Press, 2004.

Moriarty, John, *A Guide to Birding Ramsey County*, St. Paul: Ramsey County Parks and Recreation Department, St. Paul Audubon Society, 2006.

Tekiela, Stan, *Birds of Minnesota: Field Guide, Second Edition*, Cambridge: Adventure Publications, 2004.

Tekiela, Stan, *Mammals of Minnesota: Field Guide*, Cambridge: Adventure Publications, 2005.

Tekiela, Stan, *Trees of Minnesota: Field Guide*, Cambridge: Adventure Publications, 2001.

Tekiela, Stan, *Wildflowers of Minnesota: Field Guide*, Cambridge: Adventure Publications, 1999.

Vogels, Vicky, project coordinator, *Twin Cities Birding Map*, Minneapolis: Little Transport Press, 2002.

INDEX

Notes

ABOUT THE AUTHOR

This is Kate Havelin's sixteenth book. In 2007, the Midwest Independent Publishers Association chose her book *Minnesota Running Trails: Dirt, Gravel, Rocks and Roots* as the Best Sports Travel and Recreation Book in the twelve-state region. Havelin's other books include junior high biographies of Che Guevara, Queen Elizabeth I, Ulysses Grant, and Victoria Woodhull. She lives in St. Paul with her husband and two teenage sons.